TSUNAMI DIORAMA

D1036608

TSUNAMI DIORAMA

Fritz Ward

THE WORD WORKS
Washington, D.C.

FIRST EDITION
Tsunami Diorama
Copyright © 2017 by Fritz Ward

Re -pro- duction
of any part of
this book in any
form or by any means,
electronic or mechanical,
except when quoted in part
for the purpose of review, must have
written permission from the publisher.
Please address all such inquiries to us at
THE WORD WORKS P.O. Box 42164 Washington, D.C., 20015
or editor@wordworksbooks.org. Cover design: Susan Pearce Design.
Cover art: Gabriela Ferreira / Author Photo: Roxanne Halpine Ward

ISBN: 978-1-944585-11-2
LCCN: 2016962792

Acknowledgements

The following poems (or earlier versions) first appeared in various publications and are reprinted here with thanks:

American Letters and Commentary: "My Doppelgänger's Descant"
Arts & Letters: "Love Letter About to Be Lit"
Another Chicago Magazine: "Love Letter Rattling the Bell Jar"
Anti-: "Self-Portrait in Conway, Arkansas"
A Bad Penny Review: "Instructions for Burying K"
Best New Poets 2007: "Grief Is Simple Interference: Endings Overlapping"
Blackbird: "Slipknot: Starlight"
Coconut: "My Doppelgänger's John Wayne"
The Collagist: "Reenactment As America's Most Wanted #48"
Columbia Journal: "Parenthetical, Half-Dressed"
DIAGRAM: "Handbell Choir in Triage," "Letter of Relativity,"
        "Let Her," & "Dear"
diode: "Counterseduction"
ellipses: "Postcard with Tomorrow's Phobia (Yellowstone – 1978,
        Anonymous)"
Good Foot: "Postcard with Tomorrow's Phobia (Great Wave Off
        Kanagawa, Katsushika Hokusai)"
Gulf Coast: "Love Letter Committing Some Other Crime"
Handsome: "Love Letter Lingering Inside a Semi-Historical Room"
The Journal: "Shooting Range Silhouette in the Shape of a Love Letter"
Lyric: "Postcard with Tomorrow's Phobia (Japanese Garden)"
Lo-Ball: "Love Letter Where I Am Someone Else"
Memorious: "Grief Is Simple Interference: Endings Overlapping"
Nidus: "Yes, Your Mother Is"
No Tell Motel: "Love Letter Relinquishing the Articulate Veneer"
        & "Love Letter with Small Town Convulsions"
Pool: "Descant"
Portland Review: "If You Want"
Quarterly West: "Multiple Exposure with My Doppelgänger"
Salt Hill: "Postcard with Tomorrow's Phobia (Ruptured Shade, C. Berry)"
        & "Dear Cannibal Quivering with Lipstick and Moonlight"
Santa Clara Review: "Rites"

Small Spiral Notebook: "Postcard with Tomorrow's Phobia
            (Traveling on Beautiful I-80, John Penrod)"
The Southeast Review: "Dear Audoboness"
Southern Poetry Review: "Missives from the Second New Moon"
Third Coast: "Translation of the Coroner, Post-Shooting"
Tuesday; An Art Project: "Requiem for My Doppelgänger
            (Without Credits)"
Tupelo Quarterly: "Marriage"
Verse Daily: "Dear Audoboness"
42opus: "Love Letter with Tsunami Diorama"

My deep thanks to Nancy White and the wonderful team at The
Word Works for believing in this book. It also wouldn't exist without
the love and friendship of my fellow writers, including Simeon Berry,
Heather Hughes, Cecily Iddings, Adam Day, Christina Stoddard,
Emily Stenberg, Todd McKinney, Stacy Clovis Woofter, Alicia
Mooney-Flynt, Renee Soto, Dan Albergotti, Elan Young, Jill
Alexander Essbaum Peng, Rebecca Lehmann, Jennifer Chapis,
Hillary Katz, Holly Virginia-Clark, Ryan Nance, Joshua Gottlieb-
Miller, Jay Nebel, Jay Baron Nicorvo, and Erin Lavelle.

I am grateful for the guidance and support of all my teachers who
influenced the development of this manuscript, especially Stuart
Dischell, Fred Chappell, Christine Garren, Claudia Emerson, Scott
Ward, and Sterling Watson. Thanks to Jim Clark, Terry Kennedy,
and the rest of the UNCG crew for welcoming me into
a community of writers—and for the barbecue.

A lifetime of thanks to my family—Denise Ward, Fritz Ward, and
Megan Rieger—for their love, encouragement, and understanding.

Finally, thank you to my wife, Roxanne Halpine Ward, for your
unwavering love, belief, and support—and for your laugh.

And although most of the poems in this book are older than you,
thank you, Freya, for your joy and mischief.

Contents

TSUNAMI
DIORAMA

Slipknot: Starlight

This is the forest fire of thirty-five. Part smoke jumper,
part smoke. All the silver fillings in my mouth have melted.

I've set this narrative to burn down your front door. It burns blond with
        centerfolds,
blue with feverish babies. Both flames stitched together with won't.

—There, I've tried. That's all I want to remember. Now I'm starting over:
The air is shallow as an anorexic's mirror. Gray clouds. White barn.

The road overcast with feathers. Death only a Buick away. I brake
for the oblique meaning before it burns off like morning fog. I'm trying

to see something naked through the ascetic's light: a thumbnail
freckled with blood, a clear pane of rose water. I'm so close to home,

I can smell the dried mint over my mother's bed. My childhood happens
like this: A mortician's assistant sets the table with tarnished silverware.

The forks all wrong, the knives remaining. Someone dies. Or rather,
        no one dies
and we go poor. I conceive the smallest prayers walking home from
        the bus stop:

Let the cold be cold, and let it be quiet. Not even the wind to carry their cries.

And then a summer washing rented cars and reading only the endings of
        famous books.
On Van Buren Lane, the tar bubbles and bursts. Farther out, beyond the Evans

of that City, the streets are sub-atomic colliders, Medusaean waterways,
        statues sleeping.
I listen for car crashes on the police scanner. A game of restraint. A game
        of velocity

and heirloom bone structure. I listen to save someone else, someone other.
Lightning flirts. Thunder stumbles, and arrives. The rain is four minutes.

By fall, the order of events no longer mattered. The maple leaves ransom
        their colors
for warmth. It's all kindling until I meet K next to a vase of freeze-dried lilies.

K: my neologism, my netherworld nurse, all ether and eye shadow. She began
by sliding a wine cork into her pocket, saying, *I always feel more alone*

in a crowded room. We met at my aunt's funeral, where the dead were inevitable
and unsexy. She was twenty going on twilight—a little S and more

than a little M. But it was her seizures, undressed in the exact violence
of light that made me hold her down in the dark. Inside K, I was dusk

with an ashen vintage. I cindered every which way. At our wedding,
I admired all the hypochondriac pastels, each dress minted green

with envy, with luck. The wine was from Paris,
Indiana, the rice from Des Moines. We thanked everyone for the gifts

so easily divided. My childhood ended like this: Bloodroot, Trillium, Bull Thistle.
I've told you almost nothing, but don't worry, there's still time

to show all the scenery, haunted and revisionist. I could tell you anything
before the slipknot of starlight closed. Watch:

      This is the light,
      this is the steeple,
      tighten it
      here
      and choke
      all the people.

I'm tired of meaning what I almost say. Sick of grief turning intelligible near the end. This started off as a way to endure everything:

Added breath. The assonance of a moan. Seventh degree burns. Couldn't it be more than a death knell beside an unmade bed?

Couldn't it—for a moment—be the moon's dress of embezzled light? All reflection. All dust. Soon it will be Thursday again, a street sweeper

polishing the pavement, clouds suspended above like overcast hosannas. The cornflowers against the fence are never as blue as I remember.

Dear

At the end of love there is a stove.

At the end of suffering a snowman naked down to the charcoal briquettes.

At the end of earth a shower drain tangled with black hair.

At the end of day an electric fence crackling in the rain.

At the end of night a runway from which all dreams depart.

At the end of death clarified butter.

At the end of sky a space. At the end of space a wishing well.

At the end of all beginnings a door like any other, dividing inside from out.

If You Want

If you want to believe
there's a fox and a farmhouse,
go ahead. There's nothing
I can say to stop you.
But there's an old man too,

a gray husk watching
the fox's tail waver
through the broken stalks of corn:
a splash of red wine
in a field of effigies.

Look up, and the trees
smolder in spirals
above the house. Walk in,
and the floorboards sigh
with hunger, the dust parts

in small waves with each step.
The snow will not come in.
His cough, jagged and loud,
lures you down the hallway.

Go.

The door is a window
when you open it.
You want him to be your farther,
your father, your far enough.

Squint hard enough and you see
the fox's tail burns a hole
through dusk. *There*, he'll point—

But don't tell him. He knows
the fox is a woman or a thief
or himself night after night in 1983.
Oh how we hump and shit and kill

and ask forgiveness. How we hold
his shivering hand in ours
like a letter in another language, only to wake
in the morning with footprints
instead of a name,
a belly slick with mud,
a stomach full
of bones.

Postcard with Tomorrow's Phobia

(*Ruptured Shade,* C. Berry)

[Front]

> Crimson on crimson. Two calla lilies
> in the corner. Muddy. Smudged
> with a black hoofprint. Shallow.
> Edging out more abstract flowers
> than you can count.

[Back]

> My face is not a map to the Old World.
> No relief. At the south end of town:
> my instincts carved into elm trees,
> my intentions refused on lined paper
> in a landfill. You must remember weeping.
> Weather-beaten. Bruised. I am neither.

Love Letter Inside a Tsunami Diorama

Here it is:
the ocean

rising up.
So much larger

than me,
than you.

Everything
we love

miniaturized.
I cut a hole

in the side
for your eye.

When your hands
hold what I've made

they become
the waves

about to
crush it.

Grief Is Simple Interference:
Endings Overlapping

I feed the ants before I poison them.

I wrap my grief in tinsel and call the funeral director

Sugarbeets. I want to spoon her in two. One for now,

one for never. Does it matter who D-I-E-D?

After the service, there's sex and crackers and crushed

fruit. Her father snapped black and whites

of all the lilies in the room. Graveside, we shoe-gazed

and eavesdropped—palm-sized birds and the threat

of afternoon rain. *Touch me now*, she said,

I'll freckle and tear.

Multiple Exposure with My Doppelgänger

We dipped our sun-blistered hands
into these once-washed prayers. Then, faithfully,
unwashed, unclasped, and unthought

the following: *Jesus is no Pittsburgh.*
The swink of it made us queasy and unable
to enunciate. We tried standing monolithically still,

like a slurry-gray steel mill abandoned
along the shores of the Monongahela: We failed.
Whatever minor understandings we smuggled

into our thirties became pesos to place over the eyes
of roadkill. Our heart idled at the drive-through.
We ordered less than we desired. Even the words

mattered less now than the vibrations
we teased from our lover's throat.
Once upon a time, it was all terminal:

the marshgrass and the yarnbirds and the Sunshine
Skyway Bridge. We stood there, shirtless—
a camera at arm's length, snapping myself in half.

Yes, Your Mother Is

dying, your father is
dead. The bed pan in the corner
collects dust and dirty pennies.
We are seventeen—

the world is so fictionless,
algae clots the backyard pond
your father built in a bout
of alcoholic insight. It's July,

season of drought and delinquency,
the month with the most amputations.
Your fingers flirt with a yellow strand
of frayed sunlight on your ankle

as I try to coax your tears into my hand,
then maybe the smooth stones of your hips.
I imagine your mother's last breath
fleeing the boxcar of her body—

how afterwards, my breath will be the Bible
you turn to. Outside, a tire fire burns
a veil of film noir nostalgia—the late gray
caught in your throat, a lesson in asthmatic

synesthesia. Waiting for sorrow
to unravel your summer dress
into my hands, I look up *benign, malignant,*
metastasize. I thought my devotion

would short out the lamps in your room,
leaving us alone in the handmade dark,
where finally I could give up
this counterfeit cure.

Handbell Choir in Triage

First, a toast to dirty martinis
in blue plastic cups.

To the church
of unfolded hands.

To each mouth,
a scar that opens

and opens
in guttural prayer.

Then cut to the interior
with sudden bleeding.

To the tallow tongue,
the brain wick, the heart smear—

all candled into a Wichita stitch
of honeymooned light.

To the highway
hyphenated with dried blood.

To the stitch and moan,
the stifle and burn,

the stop, drop, and weep.
The ringing.

Postcard with Tomorrow's Phobia

(*Traveling on Beautiful I-80*, John Penrod)

[Front]

> The Goodyear of Asphalt leads East,
> then West, four lanes invoking the anti-
> depressant destination. In the distance, a barn
> implies the pastoral with its one red dress.
> A cow poses near a sycamore tree. The median
> feigns authority with its crew cut
> of green, its division of labor
> and accidents. Up ahead there's an exit
> simplified with arrows.

[Back]

> Last week: sadness like a sod farmer's.
> But you were never the grass—steady, faithful,
> relentless. Still, your thirst always came
> first. Like a glory hole is to a hello.
> > *Hello—*
> If it rains at all this month, I'll harvest
> a handful of mud and mold a mask
> of your face—delirious and wet.

Parenthetical, Half-Dressed

Here's the first person, no strings
attached. Here's the *I* in a jar

of formaldehyde above an unmade bed
and a narrator dressed in ellipses.

I'm here to say it's too late,
I'm tangled in this story's leather fringe.

Peach moonshine and a ghostly toast
compose the present tense. A storm idles

overhead like a stretch limousine
outside the only nightclub

in Waco, Texas—a way of saying,
lights out, no promises.

I need you to explain the blond bruise
in the white tank top

before she straightens her bra strap
and starts singing the refrain

to the beta bluegrass release
of *Precipitous Woman.*

Tell me again about the trees
bent with my longing.

The lamp's shawl of yellow light
pressed to the window.

This time, I'm letting you stand
for all of it—the choke

cherries and the stitches. The honey,
the havoc, and the grief. The made.

The unmade. The tinder-
sweet. Now tell me again

how the parentheses stand for everything
I want to love.

Counterseduction

I'm kittens, you're gravy.
My sugared rhubarb, your bone
barrettes. Together, we're the black-
berry stains on the body
bag. I make a bumble bee
of my bumbling
next to your flaming
family tree. This stinger
is a death threat
for one of us.
Remember the bullets
buzzing past our heads
when we were alive
enough to hear them?
Yes, love is the mess
we make of it. But summer
is so flammable
that when we drive to the levee
all I do is drink the lake
inside of you dry
and then turn up the radio.
Inside the glove box
is a cigar box. Inside
the cigar box an emergency
wishbone. Let's try to break
each other first. We'll start
by pretending not to care
so much. We'll invent
the gas mask, then the scarecrow.
We'll hang both from the rafters
of your father's barn, hang them
with so much care that we'll give them

pet names and then pets
and then we'll learn, finally,
how to take care
of each other.

Shooting Range Silhouette
in the Shape of a Love Letter

Dear Tinderbox of Texas Excess, how many ways can you wreck us? Your church bells and your hurricanes, your two-armed tornadoes, your smokestack of ghost-faced bats, your ten-gallon mouth. Houston. Oh, goddamned Houston. We take aim and say it. Because we can't keep what's inside us alive. For long. For never. Because the ghost towns still standing are named Swastika, Welfare, Devil's River. Because the porch is bird-shit white and we sit for hours trying to persuade each other. The wind chimes are a handful of snakeskins your father hammered to the eaves. When the storm finally arrives, we lay awake listening to the rattle of what's passing.

Translation of the Coroner, Post-Shooting

Two women kiss
their daughter's forehead
in the morgue. The organ

scale gleams like a treasure
that should be salvaged.
But the girl, the rain, the list

of words folded in her pocket—
porcelain, guava, scapula.
The coroner embraces

her frostbitten lips,
                    her snow-
softened hands. His heart

and its hoofbeats steaming
in the frozen field.
And the women hear it too—

a broken gallop
through the afterpastures.
One of us must undress

her—if only to see the fruit
beneath the amniotic
snow, to see what lies

beneath us and to offer
it our most truthful names:
driftbone, bloodseed, gut thistle.

Rites

The voodoo doll
sleeps like the future

inside the buttoned mouth
of my back pocket.

Her flesh and bones
all flour. Her skin

finger-pricked.
The mouth

a crooked stitch
of boiled leather.

The eyes thumbprints
of volcanic ash.

At the bottom
of the stairs, the clocks

draped in white.
In the mirror behind

the door,
I am twice as far.

Your descent
down the staircase

is a needle
humming in my ear.

Love Letter with Small Town Convulsions

Dear Lurid Gospel, while the park/drive-in/motor lodge/bait shop/church/post office/slaughterhouse/airport/museum/ diner / warehouse / hospital / crematorium / classroom / confessional became quieter and haunted, my sister sat on the porch swing smoking something white and marvelously addictive. *Every pain has its Rothko*, she declared. I nodded. The creek babbled obscurities back to us. The faint stars were charged with more impossibility than I cared to count. Together we watched the leaves shake free from the diseased trees.

Postcard with Tomorrow's Phobia

(Japanese Garden)

[Front]

A pond no larger than your concept
of heaven. The shadowy-orange shapes
of koi.
            A tree so small and sculpted
it's someone's child. And stones.
Always stones near the water. And light,
with all its blinding accusations.

[Back]

There are too many answers.
None of them completely right.
If there were one I could catch
in my mouth, it would be winter again,
the whole garden transcribed in white.
Only the braille of our bodies
to translate.

Letter with Retroactivity

In the triangle of dust and dead insects,
we divide your mother's memories
into boxes, choosing what to keep
and what to forget in the name of charity.

The spiders have all gone, leaving
behind their stories of tension and symmetry,
so when the web breaks across my face,
I'm already thinking about the past:

the year before I bought you the ring
and its colorless stone endlessly refracting
the light; before the radiation
licked your mother's bone marrow clean;

before the evening of broken rain
against windows, the yellow light
from her bedroom spilling into the hallway.
　　　　—It doesn't matter how I got there.
It was her bed. Her yes—my yes.
　　　　　　　　　　Yes. I counted
the silence between the lightning strands
and the web of thunder.

And then the storm was over,
the eye two miles off,
her panties crushed
like a white flag beneath us.

So if I lean toward you to steal
a kiss now, it will taste like hers,
that coda of wild ginger and mint
I will never give back.

Love Letter Relinquishing
the Articulate Veneer

Dear Fill-In-My-Blanks, my heart is a hotel room overlooking an alley bright with rain: a metal pull-chain, an empty socket, light blue curtains singed with the approximation of a human soul. The truth is this is not the truth I counted on. These fingers were not the fingers I counted on. The mattress in the corner is spare and empty. Underneath, I've hidden a book of matches and two flammable confessions. One where the grim silk grows red into the merchandise of love. One where everything I say smolders.

Descant

Februarian gray and brandied, the cloud cover
unmistakably depressing. I wander

half a block from your open window,
half wondering if my psychiatrist's id

will forgive me. Finally, closer than the closest cross
street, I stop to let my ache salivate.

If I see your sweet and slow-waltzing face
high on the shingles, I promise, I'll play coy—

not like the fish, but like the French
films with their black scarves and split-ends.

~

Okay, okay.   ~   ~ Oh K : let's say
you were ten years older. Good—

Now teach me how to undress in a poem.
When I'm nude, I'm new, I'm un-

slipped and lipped. You should stare
and I should star. Yes, stare close

enough and I'm a lily that lends
to unending bending. I've never been won,

but one that is too. Too swivel-
hipped. Two divided lips. Too little

chapstick to make the wind
really wonder what would happen.

~

Much, much later: a brunch, a bunch
of crumbs on the tongue. After toast,

the old one-two strophe. O we tarry
and we t(h)rust. We tinker

with the tips of barely known things.
You want to say *love* already, don't you?

Don't.
Now do.

Go ahead, say it with one lump,
then two. A hump is sugar cubed.

I liked the dead ants on your windowsill
best—how they curled into small black commas,

delicate as our punctuation could get.

My Doppelgänger's Descant

Beneath the cloud-loud sky,
lackbirds filled the gaps
on the telephone wire and you knocked
the pathos plant off the porch.

You tap-tap-tapped on my white-
washed door. I simply unlocked—
dropped the romance novel I was
reading—floored the bodice and the throb.

No more paper cuts for my pulp heart—
for my cult art. Was I the ark
you were praying for? Wait—
Let me be X

and let me be plain: I'm a hangnail
on a forged suicide note. I'm years older
than the artifice, a shade tree younger
than the recanting. I mean,

don't you want to decant too?
With the moon at half-mast
already half-past our half-lives,
can you really say no to me?

We'll light some sparklers
along the way, we'll burnish
our skin with one tri-colored bruise
after another, revelry ad nauseam.

If you stare close enough, my face
is a thousand black holes,
an abandoned planetarium, a hum
and a hush and a binge. Quick! Quick!

You be the lush, I'll be the hinge.
Now, thrush! Thrush! O clamor
and button, I'm coming, I'm coming.
I come with wet hands and no final answers.

If you ask twice, I'll raise my bare arms in surrender,
like an orchard emptied of its apples.

Postcard with Tomorrow's Phobia

(Hermosa Pier, California)

[Front]

> Out on the shallow sea of blue-green,
> the sailboats swarm like insects, scuttering just so.
> The clouds smudge one off-white thought
> into the next, and the black-dash birds soar, bodiless,
> over the arc of splinters.

[Back]

> When you dip your fingers
> into the ocean
> and stick them in my mouth,
> I pray and prey. I swallow
> the angels all over again.
> All that wet begging—
> We're worth it, right?

Dear Cannibal Quivering
with Lipstick and Moonlight

I was nominally yours. You were abnormally mine. We loved with fangs
out, truths in. I licked fifty-six square inches of your lavendered skin. I begged

for the first two psalms and received your twenty-four hour flood. I listened
        for your
three deepest breaths, but your mouth was a drain painted *Harlot*. You
        hand-washed

six figs, fed me one per night. And each of those meals in between, I longed
for your ingredients: your sweet cream and your curry and your overripe bed.

And I stayed, not for the cancer or your skin beneath me, but to watch
        your soft hands
flutter and flay the green skin of the mango, its glistening exposed, alone.

That spring delivered the first four steps of happiness and I tangoed in
        the mineshafts
of your moonlight, unsutured. Summer sent us your slow-clotting cuts,
        your sugar ants,

your human dark and your wild honey. It was all a little too sweet to believe in.

Letter of Relativity

Let's be honest: The sun's sermon
of starlight is too much. The three grains of rock salt
dissolving on the ice-covered street reveal nothing
about devotion. Often enough, love is weaker

than gravity. Now let's be dishonest:
Here, I'll offer you this vision of a cardinal
stationed in the pin oak, a red ransom note
illuminating the window, desire incognito.

Feathered red and sprinkled with lice,
the metaphor is marked for illness, for a hospital window
painted shut in Syracuse. Watch the patient
as she watches a nest of crooked twigs

and gray string slowly untangle.
I want an alley of snow and cigarette butts
beyond the oak tree. A man with six coats
pissing his initials into the hour-old snow.

He'll explain the evolution
of parking garages: How the exhaust
gathering in the corners translates into a warmth
that lingers till midnight. The man is a flower-

potted drunk. He adorns the alley.
The leaves of his hands unfold for loose change.
But maybe I want to keep this season of self-deception:
leaves resurrecting the hills, a red metaphor on a gray branch,

the therapy of acid rain seeping
into the basement, flooding the family portraits
of discontent—flooding my life with honesty,
which was only ankle-deep to begin with,

barely deep enough for the drowning. But the truth is less convincing than snow, and the truth is, I want to hurt you. Just a little. Just enough to make you turn this page and lie with me a little longer.

Love Letter About to Be Lit

Dear Incendiary Saint, a house fire
        is a hypnotist with beauty to spare.
                But having burned once before, this time

                I wanted the smoke to stand in for the soul
        ascending. Of course, it was always a screen,
an alibi, a full-length feature for our improvised

truths. When the yellow firemen finally
        arrived, I watched your pale neck ignite
                as they waved to you from inside their movie-

                sized coats. You opened wide and caught the ashes
        on your tongue while an ember burned slowly
through the hem of your engine-red nightgown.

In the morning, I confessed to all
        the love letters I should have written you:
                Cinder, sunburn, surrender.

Missives from the Second New Moon

I couldn't commit your name
to ink or air
for seven days

I swallowed two magnets
one for the ice storm
one for the arson

Despite a dram of mercury
I've received no message
only the myth of you

You are two rivers of salt
and one minute
of distilled moonlight

You crush a clove of garlic
with the knife's gleaming flank
The white dress of desire hanging
from your shoulders

What am I to make of the solstice
without your skin dying next to me
gathering itself into piles of dust
beneath the bed

The first letter never left the dogstar

The second is dipped in gasoline

But the third
the third shivers now
in the mail carrier's hands

Postcard with Tomorrow's Phobia

(*Yellowstone – 1978*, Anonymous)

[Front]

> Ash-black and mulberry—Stump
> and pine—Purpled wren—The confusion
> of February—Berries veiled beneath
> the paint of snow—Shadows green
> at the fringe—The sun entirely missing—

[Back]

> When I hit the dog, I thought only
> of you—how your hands made a trellis
> of your face when you cried. I asked
> for more, but dusk came—narcotic and quick.
> And then the dog rose—slowly—
> all limps and whimpers. My heart idled.
> I made a shovel with these hands.

Reenactment as America's
Most Wanted #48

You're just his stand-in.

You're the man that makes the ficus
by the bay window look less loved.

You simulate a bare yellow bulb
and strategic cobwebs, cinder blocks

and composite crooks, genuine
poverty. You stand just

so.

If you stare at a wallet-size reproduction
of his face, you can make your eyes like ice

over an orange grove. If the director desires
your nose closer to your lips, you conform,

you transpire. When you achieve him—
the electrical fire and locust—

there's no feeling to mimic it,
a faux gun in your man's hand

and the left side of our mockingbird
brain falling fast asleep:

Take twenty-one.
Take twenty-two.

We move the massacre
to the foreground. The children learn

how to fall into their shadows.
Shhhh, you're only here to hurry the rain

into my heart.

Letter, Clip

If you go back far enough in my family tree there are birds.
—Susan Mitchell

1.
Susan, if I had your ovaries,
I'd summon a homing pigeon

to deliver the plague. I'd sweep
feathers from the sidewalk

until I had a coffin or a pillow.
It's not that I want you

dead, but yesterday, lying
on a picnic table

at a rest stop in Virginia,
all those syndicated symbols

of hope flocked straight
to a forest of Dutch Elm disease.

2.
Susan, when I was you,
I let my breasts dangle.

I let the sand crabs creep
across my painted toes.

I asked the moon to drop
her stole of embittered light

so as to lead no one else astray.
For moral support,

I strung a hammock
between pine trees—

a family of nooses
holding hands.

3.
Susan, high in the canopy,
a warbler sings and spreads

its communicable disease.
Below, pine needles

stifle the undergrowth.
Yesterday, I left my hollow

bones in the womb.
Today, I stand enormously

still. Like the ash tree
shading the crematorium,

I willow, but I cannot weep.

4.
Susan, if I am God,
there are so many reasons

to worry. All I ask
is that you suffer

with me.

Love Letter Committing
Some Other Crime

Dear 1989, the definition of happiness is a tiny human knot. To mimic the man I want to be again, I imagine the shipwreck of your voice inventing me. A hum and a howl and a suture. Never were we the children we imagined ourselves. In a chamber of my heart, there's a black bear and a bee. Honey, can you trust me again? Until that midnight, let these crimes suffice: the choke-damp grass, your sunburned thighs, a postcard of the last white buffalo. Come here with all that sadness.

Marriage

1.
But no one tells that story
any longer. That story is a bear
trap glazed with rust and boar's blood.
This poem is the skin of the salmon
drizzled with honey and salt
served in a moonlit Havahart.

2.
This is the night we lay
our heavy heads on feather-dead
pillows and listen to the raccoons
making a life of our attic. In the heavens
between our hungers and theirs,
you keep breathing
the best parts of midnight,
leaving me only the scat of stars.

3.
Baited with the paw
of a snow fox the color
of your finest lingerie
and the last slice
of raspberry pie—your heart,
that trap, waiting to snap.

4.
If I let my sheep loose,
can I trust your animal
instincts? If I call
the carrion home,
will you sing
the butcher's song

come morning?
Tell me again how
delicate your snares.
How they snaked
for months through
the weathered seasons
just to graze a bare ankle.

5.
If I promised you
two truths, then keep
reading me.
One: When I scream
your name,
I mean to spook
all the beasts
but you.
Two: If no one tells
our story, then we
haven't failed
               enough.

My Doppelgänger's John Wayne

He's all Mojave. All that sweat
and sand. All those sunsets.

He's swift to sear, but slow to blow
the candles out. His grit scours

the tongue in the sweat lodge of my mouth.
Like a cactus, he pricks

to protect the water inside.
He squints and testifies.

He leans against the unblinking sun
for support. I stare and go, go, go

blind as the Joshua tree.
His Western-wear and diamond-backed

fingers rattle across my cheek.
I'm all pilgrim: already bitten,

already pale, all ready
for the ending where I lie down

with this body and make an angel
in the sand of his death valley.

Love Letter Where I Am Someone Else

Dear Exterior, when I stumbled through your corn husks and hay bars
and the whine of your caesarean guitars,

I rendered the past *a senseless tense.* Even the border guards blinked as sparse
parts for the incinerator rumbled past. Fall arrived and arrived

and departed. The leaves shadowed and scratched. I listened. To the guard's
thin whistle as he snapped the heads of sweet alyssum for his sleeping
wife. She lived.

A quiet life. Outside, everyone was. Smoking. Three inches
taller. The religious significance almost laryngitic. When I arrived, *almost*

undressed was still best. Thank you, substance. Thank you,
tinder. I spent a long time. Forgetting. Today, I refuse to speak

of her beauty, her bread. The children were never immortal,
only less sad. A napkin marked with dried blood was an angel.

Still, my Dresden is nothing like her Dresden.

Dear Auduboness

The silence between us is measured
in dead birds.
           I've taken my scarecrow
           mask off to say
I'm sorry for this ending
with insects.
           In our Scranton, the reflection
           of the truth
is worth the dying for.
This morning,
           the cardinals sang *purdy-purdy*
           whoit-whoit
before flying into the glass echo
of themselves.
           From the frost-tipped grass,
           I count the blond
wisps of hair over the backs of your hands
through the window.
           If I were the right kind
           of lover, this poem
would have less death
in it—birds stunned,
           not broken. But gloved
           and shoveled, I raise
each body to your framed face, praying
you'll break the window,
           my goddamned heart.

Postcard with Tomorrow's Phobia

(*Mendocino Cliff*, J. Ambry)

[Front]

> What passes for the sky is a burial at sea.
> Below that, trees shoulder the horizon,
> a stone poses as a thought too gray to lift.
> Wind curves the long blades of grass
> back to earth. The cliff's sheer
> devotion to the waves is crumbling.

[Back]

> The malignant flowers.
> The estuary mud.
> The rain hurrying us
> inside. Then night's
> viscera glistening.
> Our antlers on the floor.
> Our furred feet chained
> to luck, then the rearview.
>   *Come back, my dear.*
> Not to remember,
> but to dismember the rest
>   of us.

Love Letter with Tsunami Diorama

Dear Petite Violence, after she left, I found the Collins glass of table wine on the windowsill. It counterweighed the nightbird's absence. After she left the second time, I lit a candle in our churchyard and played undertaker, thinking I could take her under me. So I pressed my ear to the shell of her absence. There was an ocean where her voice had been.

Requiem for My Doppelgänger
(Without Credits)

It doesn't matter how the bullets
got from Smith to Wesson

to this noir-lit kitchen,
or how we moved

from Disneyland
to The Mattress Factory

to the ransacked jewelry box
of her heart.

It was all one funeral
viewed from the fire ant's

perspective: dark shoes,
loose earth.

This is how we work:
We break our body

for the dirt.

Love Letter Lingering
Inside a Semi-Historical Room

Dear Confederate Docent, what do we do with all the spare Southern scenery? The ice cream and incest. The peach and its shadow. It's August on your skin, but tell me again about the men in that cornfield, the ones belly-crawling between the dandelions and the dead. I've never held a gun, but when I let the muzzle of my trigger finger graze your almond-colored wrist, I start praying for the secession of your habitual hem, imagining the sounds of our union. My fisted heart keeps pounding, but the rain-strange windows of this semi-historical room were painted shut in 1923. One steeple north of your lavender dress, my grandmother married an undertaker from Blacksburg. It rained for seven nights. The cornfield became a shallow sea he ferried her across: Frederick carrying Dorothy. A mouthful of sky. The thorn you kiss goodnight. The kind of prayer you bury beneath the rose bush. They are the bodies between these churches. We are the stain upon the glass.

Postcard with Tomorrow's Phobia

(Fargo, ND – Sunflower Capital of the U.S.)

[Front]

> Field sick with sun and flower. Faces filled
> with seeds. The sky touched blue, then bluer,
> then drowned. The trees at a distance, nameless
> and anonymous, a green defining the horizon.

[Back]

> It's night now. Winter. Snow
>   like chewed feathers
> over the empty field.
>   I remember the first illness—
> that paradise
>   of need you gave   and gave
> and gave
>   till one of us
>   was gone.

Instructions for Burying K

Startle the winter bees
and wake the coffined

angels. Carve her name
into the first fallen tree

and call it elegy.
Wait for the woodthrush,

but not the flood.
Shroud her bed

with the violence
of all those freshly cut

flowers. She was hymn
and hive and raw

honey. She could kill
a child. Then climb in.

Self-Portrait in Conway, Arkansas

A cloud drags its clubfoot
over the bare sky. The damp grass

imparts subtle, changing
secrets. The cows amble black and white.

This need to see and not be seen
through. Beneath the barbwire's string

of thin infinities, a fist of daisies
wilts beneath a jaundiced ribbon.

I've come without a god
or a tow truck. The gravel so loose

and plural, I fill my pockets
with its burden and, complicit, press my hands

to dirt. There's no comfort in the flowering
of weeds. A feeling now: wet wool

and rotting honeysuckle, a linen handkerchief
turning red in the mason's shaking hand.

So much moonlight in the flattened cornfield
we couldn't possibly go blind. I'll say it once,

and never again.

Thanks Again

I wake to the rain
falling like paper clips

against the window
and the radiator hissing

the brief friction
of atom on atom.

It's early. The dark
still dark, and you

in the shower—
all silhouette and steam.

The hot water falls
like bee wings

over you and over you
and over. I am still that boy

eager to cut his heart
into honeycomb

so that I may feed you
cell by cell.

Love Letter Rattling the Bell Jar

Dear Less-Than-Judy-Garland, love is merely a suggestion: an Oz-factory of rube-red sequins manufactured from parts of the witch's heart. Let me propose an alternative plot: a night-edged merlot, a riding crop with a clause, a mildly historical curse. Better yet, you arsoned your way across the room, past the pine needles and the holly. I widened my loneliness to include you. So very so. We gooseberried, then re-married. All afternoon, we lay in bed listening to the early recordings of rain. We floated, but still found ourselves submerged. When the listening ceased, you made a bridge of my fingers. I tore your name in half and let the river decide which vowels to drown. Oh fuck the *why*, the *what* and the *how*—Darling, this time I choose your meatloaf all over again. I choose your naked feet upon my bare chest.

Let Her

My life is a train deceiving its destination, and with its cargo of bread, blood, and ash, I meant to cross your station by now, or be stationed at your cross. But the birds haven't beaten the air into complete submission yet, and my kiss—My kiss is that of a seamstress's mending the torn. I couldn't kiss you unless it would kill you.

On my way out of Ely, I stopped at the Blue Light, but couldn't find more than a single sweating bottle of myself. When I didn't see you, I didn't see her. I knew one of you had left a note: *A woman wearing a glass of water can incite a funeral*. I sighed. As a ventriloquist for the dispossessed, it was my duty to write it on the rust-flecked mirror in the men's room.

What I had in mind was a linguistic contortionist with a cinnamon aftertaste, a dissident in black, a Dionysian in a red wig—someone to fracture my story with the simple circumference of her wrist. When I found her, she was disguised as a pediatric nurse. It was over. All I had left was to detonate the g-spot and translate the lexicon of labia into one long legato. She pushed my head down and said, *The orchid is a white fever and the body a stain we sweat away.*

There is the past: Glass-shattered. Metal-bent. Body of impact. Body of inertia. Blood spreading like wings on the asphalt.

There is always the past: Prayers to the god of anesthesiology. The needle's sutra. The white flag of her body—all the blue thread unraveling as red.

It hadn't happened yet. Everything was in the next room. Prayer was just one more erogenous zone. Yes, I'd swallowed a magnet or two and sipped some Persian blue house paint—but it wasn't always vertigo, always vice. Once, before hymn and hymen became one, before her whisper: *Orgasm is the pit of the fruit, lyricism its flesh*. But the truth is: Truth and the epidermis are individual matters, like seed and cervix, like the one she, the one you, the one epiphany of arrhythmia and freckles.

By now you know I'm not as infamous or tempting as that glass of water, nor half as gnostic as the cold front and its resurrection of rain. But some mornings, I wake and exhale with all the hypnoerotic swagger of a Raoul. The rest of the time, like any good reader, I take my clues from the weather—or from a cardinal, which possesses the same temptation as a drop of blood. Which is to say free association can get out of hand, or out of a locked hotel room without breaking a sweat or a window or one of her long, luxuriously painted nails.

The *I* is trying to say he bought a cactus in Ely, taped it to the dash and named it *post-modernism* for its one red flower, its idiom of irony. He fled. Yes, the *I* is ransacking the blood bank, stripping the smell of ammonia off a doll's lips, trying to understand a field simplified with snow—to undress the unaddressed, which is to undress himself past postmortem.

Afterwards—meaning after I'd given up on meaning—I made her one black dress entirely spectral and let it say *absence, abstinence*. I had contracted something semi-omniscient. I took the last two slivers of her fingernails left on the sink and put their affected affliction on the pillow. The bed was wholly unused. I was in. I was divisible.

Postcard with Tomorrow's Phobia

(*Great Wave off Kanagawa*, Katsushika Hokusai)

[Front]

It touches the one sky that touches everything,
even the snow on Mt. Fuji and the pale yellow
brushstrokes of the boats, the tiny faces
turned down as their oars argue with the ocean.

[Back]

This morning I drowned an ant in the sink.
I had dreamed that I was fresh from your thighs
        and you had given me a word
to say over and over, *isshuuki*,
a way to dip my tongue into the sound
and row toward you.

About the Author

Fritz Ward is the author of the chapbook *Doppelgänged* and a recipient of the Cecil Hemley Memorial Prize from the Poetry Society of America. His poetry has appeared in *American Poetry Review*, *Best New Poets*, *Blackbird*, *DIAGRAM*, *Gulf Coast*, and elsewhere. He lives just outside of Philadelphia and works at Swarthmore College.

About the Artist

Gabriela Ferreira is a painter and photographer based in Lisbon, Portugal. She graduated from the University of Fine Arts Academy of Lisbon. View more of her work at www.liebegaby.com.

OTHER WORD WORKS BOOKS

Annik Adey-Babinski, *Okay Cool No Smoking Love Pony*
Karren L. Alenier, *Wandering on the Outside*
Karren L. Alenier, ed., *Whose Woods These Are*
Christopher Bursk, ed., *Cool Fire*
Barbara Goldberg, *Berta Broadfoot and Pepin the Short*
Frannie Lindsay, *If Mercy*
Elaine Magarrell, *The Madness of Chefs*
Marilyn McCabe, *Glass Factory*
Ann Pelletier, *Letter That Never*
Ayaz Pirani, *Happy You Are Here*
W.T. Pfefferle, *My Coolest Shirt*
Jacklyn Potter, Dwaine Rieves, Gary Stein, eds., *Cabin Fever:*
    Poets at Joaquin Miller's Cabin
Robert Sargent, *Aspects of a Southern Story*
    & *A Woman from Memphis*
Fritz Ward, *Tsunami Diorama*
Amber West, *Hen & God*
Nancy White, ed., *Word for Word*

The Tenth Gate Prize

Jennifer Barber, *Works on Paper*, 2015
Roger Sedarat, *Haji as Puppet*, 2016
Lisa Sewell, *Impossible Object*, 2014

The Washington Prize

Nathalie F. Anderson, *Following Fred Astaire*, 1998
Michael Atkinson, *One Hundred Children Waiting for a Train*, 2001
Molly Bashaw, *The Whole Field Still Moving Inside It*, 2013
Carrie Bennett, *biography of water*, 2004
Peter Blair, *Last Heat*, 1999
John Bradley, *Love-in-Idleness: The Poetry of Roberto Zingarello*,
    1995, 2nd edition 2014
Christopher Bursk, *The Way Water Rubs Stone*, 1988
Richard Carr, *Ace*, 2008
Jamison Crabtree, *Rel[AM]ent*, 2014
Jessica Cuello, *Hunt*, 2016
B. K. Fischer, *St. Rage's Vault*, 2012
Linda Lee Harper, *Toward Desire*, 1995
Ann Rae Jonas, *A Diamond Is Hard But Not Tough*, 1997
Frannie Lindsay, *Mayweed*, 2009
Richard Lyons, *Fleur Carnivore*, 2005
Elaine Magarrell, *Blameless Lives*, 1991
Fred Marchant, *Tipping Point*, 1993, 2nd edition 2013
Ron Mohring, *Survivable World*, 2003
Barbara Moore, *Farewell to the Body*, 1990
Brad Richard, *Motion Studies*, 2010
Jay Rogoff, *The Cutoff*, 1994
Prartho Sereno, *Call from Paris*, 2007, 2nd edition 2013
Enid Shomer, *Stalking the Florida Panther*, 1987
John Surowiecki, *The Hat City After Men Stopped Wearing
    Hats*, 2006
Miles Waggener, *Phoenix Suites*, 2002
Charlotte Warren, *Gandhi's Lap*, 2000
Mike White, *How to Make a Bird with Two Hands*, 2011
Nancy White, *Sun, Moon, Salt*, 1992, 2nd edition 2010
George Young, *Spinoza's Mouse*, 1996

The Hilary Tham Capital Collection

Nathalie Anderson, *Stain*
Mel Belin, *Flesh That Was Chrysalis*
Carrie Bennett, *The Land Is a Painted Thing*
Doris Brody, *Judging the Distance*
Sarah Browning, *Whiskey in the Garden of Eden*
Grace Cavalieri, *Pinecrest Rest Haven*
Cheryl Clarke, *By My Precise Haircut*
Christopher Conlon, *Gilbert and Garbo in Love*
     & *Mary Falls: Requiem for Mrs. Surratt*
Donna Denizé, *Broken like Job*
W. Perry Epes, *Nothing Happened*
David Eye, *Seed*
Bernadette Geyer, *The Scabbard of Her Throat*
Barbara G. S. Hagerty, *Twinzilla*
James Hopkins, *Eight Pale Women*
Brandon Johnson, *Love's Skin*
Marilyn McCabe, *Perpetual Motion*
Judith McCombs, *The Habit of Fire*
James McEwen, *Snake Country*
Miles David Moore, *The Bears of Paris*
     & *Rollercoaster*
Kathi Morrison-Taylor, *By the Nest*
Tera Vale Ragan, *Reading the Ground*
Michael Shaffner, *The Good Opinion of Squirrels*
Maria Terrone, *The Bodies We Were Loaned*
Hilary Tham, *Bad Names for Women*
     & *Counting*
Barbara Louise Ungar, *Charlotte Brontë, You Ruined My Life*
     & *Immortal Medusa*
Jonathan Vaile, *Blue Cowboy*
Rosemary Winslow, *Green Bodies*
Michele Wolf, *Immersion*
Joe Zealberg, *Covalence*

International Editions

Kajal Ahmad (Alana Marie Levinson-LaBrosse, Mewan Nahro Said Sofi, and Darya Abdul-Karim Ali Najin, trans., with Barbara Goldberg), *Handful of Salt*

Keyne Cheshire (trans.), *Murder at Jagged Rock: A Tragedy by Sophocles*

Jean Cocteau (Mary-Sherman Willis, trans.), *Grace Notes*

Yoko Danno & James C. Hopkins, *The Blue Door*

Moshe Dor, Barbara Goldberg, Giora Leshem, eds., *The Stones Remember: Native Israeli Poets*

Moshe Dor (Barbara Goldberg, trans.), *Scorched by the Sun*

Lee Sang (Myong-Hee Kim, trans.), *Crow's Eye View: The Infamy of Lee Sang, Korean Poet*

Vladimir Levchev (Henry Taylor, trans.), *Black Book of the Endangered Species*